Scary Creatures
HIPPOS

Written by
Penny Clarke

Created and designed
by David Salariya

Author:

Penny Clarke is an author and editor
specialising in information books for children. She
has written titles on natural history, rainforests and
volcanoes, as well as others on different periods of
history. She used to live in central London, but thanks
to modern technology she has now realised her dream
of being able to live and work in the countryside.

Artists:

Janet Baker & Julian
  Baker (JB Illustrations)
John Francis
Li Sidong
Robert Morton

Series Creator:

David Salariya was born in Dundee,
Scotland. In 1989 he established The Salariya Book
Company. He has illustrated a wide range of books
and has created many new series for publishers in the
UK and overseas. He lives in Brighton with his wife,
illustrator Shirley Willis, and their son.

Editor: Tanya Kant

Editorial Assistant:
Rob Walker

Picture Research:
Mark Bergin

Photo Credits:
Dreamstime: 15
iStockphoto: 14, 17, 28
Jonathan Salariya: 4, 5, 8, 9, 13, 16, 25, 26, 27

Pygmy hippo

Published in Great Britain in 2009 by
Book House, an imprint of
The Salariya Book Company Ltd
25 Marlborough Place, Brighton BN1 1UB

SALARIYA

A catalogue record for this book is available
from the British Library.

HB ISBN: 978-1-906714-03-1
PB ISBN: 978-1-906714-04-8

Printed in China

Visit our website at **www.book-house.co.uk**
or go to **www.salariya.com** for *free* electronic
versions of:
You Wouldn't Want to be an Egyptian Mummy!
You Wouldn't Want to be a Roman Gladiator!
Avoid Joining Shackleton's Polar Expedition!
Avoid Sailing on a 19th-Century Whaling Ship!

PAPER FROM
SUSTAINABLE
FORESTS

Contents

Common hippo

What are hippos?

Hippos (short for hippopotamuses) are large **mammals**. Their name, which means 'river horse' in Greek, gives a clue about their lives. They spend most of their time swimming in African rivers and lakes or grazing along the riverbanks.

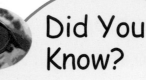

Did You Know?

Hippos have webbed toes which help them to swim well. They are good divers and can close their nostrils when they dive so that they don't breathe in water.

Hippos spend most of the day like this – almost submerged in water. They come on land to feed and bask on the riverbank.

Why are hippos scary?

Hippos are large and aggressive – that's why they're scary! They are very protective of their **territory**, and will attack anyone, human or animal, who comes near their piece of bank. The hippo in the photo above is not yawning. Opening its mouth like this to show its teeth is a warning – and a threat.

Where do hippos live?

Today there are two **species** of hippo – the pygmy hippo and the common hippo. Both live in rivers and lakes in Africa, south of the Sahara Desert. But **fossils** found by **palaeontologists** show that hippos once lived in other parts of Africa, Asia and even Europe.

Pygmy hippos now only live in a few parts of west Africa, from Guinea to Nigeria. Common hippos are more widespread. They live in east, central, and western Africa, from the edge of the Sahara Desert in the north to Namibia and the Transvaal in South Africa.

Common hippo's foot

Did You Know?

Hippos have four toes on each foot. You can see them on the feet of the hippo on the contents page.

Seen from underneath, the four toes on the foot of a hippo are very obvious. Each toe has a protective nail. As a hippo walks, its feet spread to stop it from sinking into muddy riverbanks.

Pygmy hippo's foot

This map of Africa shows where the two species of hippo live. The shaded area shows where common hippos can be found, the red areas show where pygmy hippos live.

Common hippopotamus

Pygmy hippopotamus

The rare pygmy hippo lives in rivers in the forests of Liberia, Sierra Leone and southern Nigeria.

How do hippos live?

Common hippos live in large, well-organised family groups. The oldest female leads the group. There is usually only one adult male in a group, so when young males become adults, they must leave. If they don't leave on their own, the females will chase them out.

Each hippo group has its own **crèche** – an area where female hippos take care of young hippos. The crèche is usually on the bank of a river or lake or on a sandbar in the middle of a river. The females and young gather at the crèche when they are not feeding or in the water.

These two young hippos are squaring up for a fight. When fighting, older hippos will slash at each other with their tusks, roaring and bellowing.

A crèche of young hippos gathers by the bank of the Mara River, Kenya.

How do hippos feed?

Hippos are **herbivores** – they eat only plants. Because they are such big animals, they need to eat huge amounts of plant material. Each evening, hippos leave the water and walk to where they will feed that night.

Although hippos are bigger than cows, they eat less food. This is because hippos don't need much energy to move about in the water.

Male hippos are more solitary than females and go alone to the feeding grounds. Each male has his own path and marks it with dung to warn others off.

X-Ray Vision

Hold the next page up to the light and see what's inside a hippo.

See What's Inside

Female hippos feeding on the riverbank

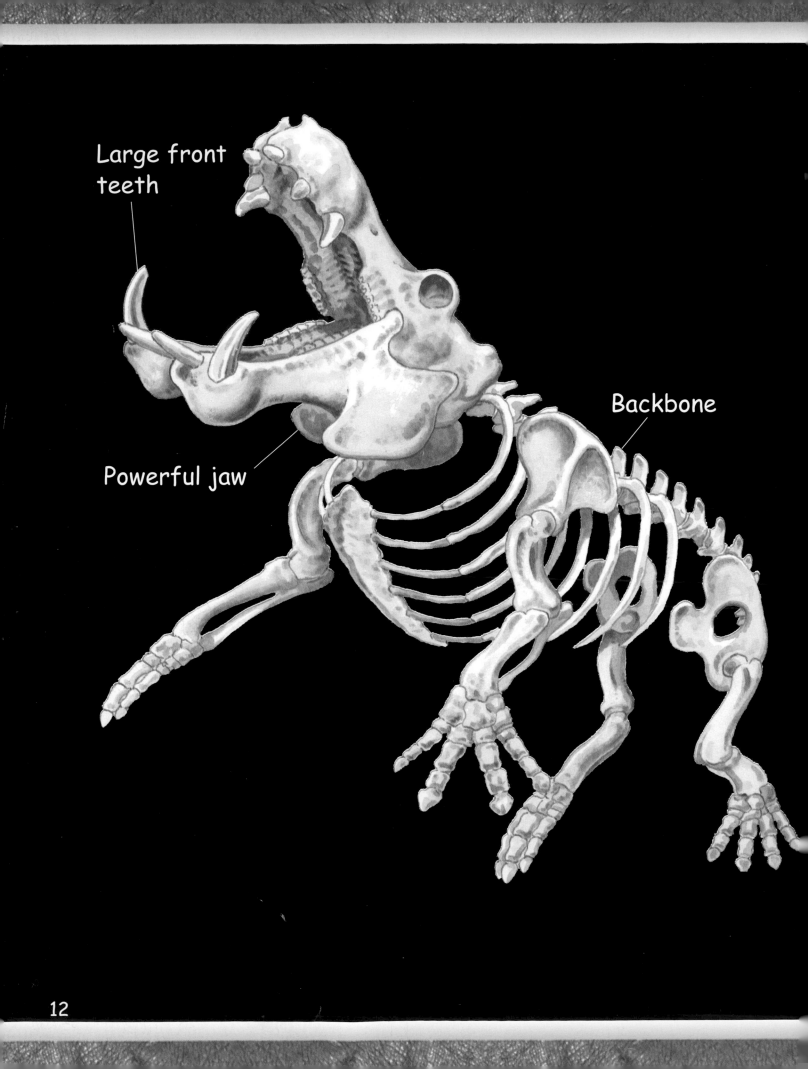

Large front teeth

Powerful jaw

Backbone

Do hippos have enough food?

Plants grow fast in the warm, wet **habitats** where hippos live, so there is usually plenty of food. Female hippos usually have their babies early in the wet season, when the heavy rainfall means that there is plenty of grass.

Did You Know?

Hippos eat grass and other plants but will also eat fruit that has fallen from trees growing along the riverbank.

Hippo grazing on the riverbank

Are all hippos huge?

No! Compared to the common hippo, pygmy hippos are very small. Adults are only about 1.9 metres long and 0.8 metre tall at the shoulder. Because they are smaller they are also much lighter: only a quarter of a tonne compared to the common hippo's 3 to 4 tonnes.

Pygmy hippos live in thick vegetation by streams flowing through the dense forests of West Africa. They rarely come into the open. Their diet includes grasses, **tubers**, fallen fruit and aquatic plants.

A pygmy hippo swims through waterweed in an African stream.

A pygmy hippo bares its teeth as a warning to an intruder – probably the photographer. They look fierce, but pygmy hippos are shy creatures that prefer to run from danger, rather than stand and fight.

Are hippos bald?

A hippo isn't completely bald, even though it may look hairless in photos like the one below. The hairiest part of a hippo is the end of its tail, but it also has hair on its chin, **muzzle** and ears. If you could stroke a hippo's chin, the hair would feel like stiff bristles.

You can just see the hairs on this hippo's muzzle.

Were hippos once hairy? Did spending so much time in water make them lose their hair? No-one knows. Instead of hair to protect their skin, hippos have a substance called 'pink sweat'.

Hairy muzzle

Hairy ears

Sometimes hippos look as if they have shiny skin. They don't. Their skin is rather dull; it's the pink sweat that gives it a shine.

Hairy chin

Pink sweat protects hippos' skin from long periods in water. It is a pink, oily substance that hippos **secrete** from special **glands** in the fatty layer under their skin.

Pink sweat

Were there ancient hippos?

Palaeontologists have found hippo fossils in north-western Europe that are around 120,000 years old. These ancient hippos looked much like the hippos alive today, except that their eyes were placed very high on their heads.

Europe 120,000 years ago

Straight-tusked elephants

Fossils can tell us what the Earth was like in the past, what plants and animals there were, what the climate was like and how it has changed.

Ancient rhino

Raised eye

Ancient hippos

Raised eyes helped ancient hippos to see clearly above the water when they swam.

Did You Know?

Hippo hunting was a favourite sport of the **pharaohs** (ancient Egyptian kings).

Nowadays, hippos don't live in the part of the River Nile that flows through Egypt, but **archaeologists** think they once did. The ancient Egyptians painted hippos on the walls of their tombs and made thousands of models of them. These little hippos date from about 2000 BC. The flowers painted on their backs represent the abundance of life that the Nile supports.

Clay model

Painted model

Hippos were a dangerous nuisance to the ancient Egyptians. Each year they killed hundreds of people, attacking and capsizing (overturning) their small boats. They also ate the crops growing in the fields beside the Nile.

Wall painting

God or monster?

In the distant past, many people believed that gods visited Earth in the shape of powerful animals. The ancient Egyptians were no exception. As hippos are powerful, dangerous animals, ancient Egyptians believed Seth, their god of evil, was a hippo.

Ancient Egyptian gods were usually painted with a human body and the head of an animal (such as Seth, the hippo) or bird (such as Thoth, the ibis).

Good or evil?

Hippos weren't always regarded as evil. Taweret, the goddess who helped Egyptian women when they were giving birth, was part hippo.

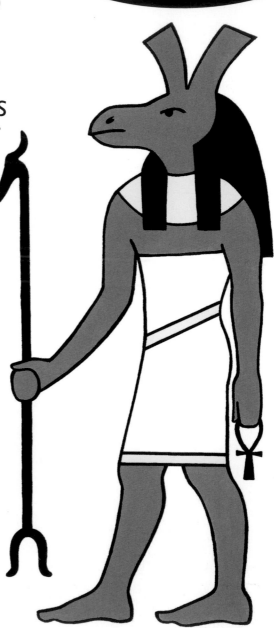

X-Ray Vision

Hold the next page up to the light to see what happens when a hippo meets an ancient Egyptian boat.

See What Happens

Ancient Egyptian god Seth

Reed fishing boat

Hunting hippos was exciting but very dangerous. Men armed with stone-tipped spears hunted hippos from fragile reed boats. Hippos were common and so were easy to find.

What was an ancient Egyptian hippo hunt like?

Ancient Egyptian wall paintings show us what hippo hunts were like. Hunters would find hippos in the waters and reed-lined areas of the Nile and hunt them from small boats made of **papyrus** reeds.

The ancient Egyptians believed their pharaoh was like a god. When he killed a hippo he was protecting his people by striking a blow against the evil god Seth.

Ancient Egyptian drawing of a hippo hunt

Do hippos have enemies?

Hippos are so large and aggressive that most animals will not risk attacking them. Occasionally lions have been seen leaping onto a hippo's back and slashing at its sides with their claws. But hippos have such tough skin that this usually does little damage. In fact, humans armed with weapons are hippos' only enemies.

Despite weighing up to 4 tonnes, adult hippos run extremely fast – around 48 kph (30 mph). If anyone gets too near to their young, a hippo will charge the intruder and will trample them if they trip and fall.

Hippos will charge anyone who comes too close.

The ancient Egyptians and other African peoples killed hippos with stone- and metal-tipped weapons. It was only when Europeans with guns reached Africa that hippos faced a serious threat.

Hippos gather in tight groups for safety.

Canine tooth

Some people collect the ivory **canine teeth** of hippos and carve them into ornaments. This puts hippos at risk of being killed just for their teeth. Is making an ornament a good reason to kill an animal?

Did You Know?

Adult hippos' canine teeth are almost a metre long. In some old males they reach 1.75 metres! Both lengths include the long roots needed to anchor such huge teeth in the skull.

Are hippos in danger?

Female hippo with her young baby swimming beside her

The greatest dangers facing hippos (apart from humans) are climate change and habitat loss. Africa has two seasons: wet and dry. By the end of the dry season, the rivers and waterholes have shrunk and many species must compete for the little remaining water. In some areas, the dry season is getting longer and less rain is falling.

The destruction of forest habitat is a serious threat to pygmy hippos because they spend less time in water than common hippos. They also hide in vegetation when threatened or frightened.

Baby hippos stay with their mothers for several years. When going to feed, the mother leads, with her babies following one behind the other, the oldest last.

Can mothers hurt their babies?

The biggest threat facing a baby hippo can be its own mother. Hippos can move fast but are really quite clumsy. Several tonnes of hippo charging into or out of the water could easily knock a baby over. Or the baby could be trodden on and crushed. Perhaps this is what happened to the young hippo below. But its death is not a waste, as its body provides food for other creatures.

Crocodile and monitor lizard approaching a dead baby hippo

Are hippos important?

Hippos are very important. They eat huge quantities of vegetation, keeping the banks clear for other creatures to reach the water. Because they eat so much, they produce enormous amounts of waste. This natural fertiliser helps sustain the **ecosystems** of the rivers and lakes in which hippos live.

Did You Know?

The tonnes of waste an adult hippo excretes each year help plants, insects and tiny water organisms to grow.

Sunlight shining through water dapples a submerged hippo's back.

Do hippos help other animals?

If hippos didn't eat waterside plants, some of the smaller creatures shown below would struggle to reach the water to drink. And the river is not just a source of water, but of food, too. Tiny **invertebrates** that thrive on hippo dung are food for fish and insects. These animals, in turn, are eaten by larger creatures – and so on up the **food chain**.

Did You Know?

In some areas, hippos eat all of the tall grass that lines the riverbank. This makes hunting difficult for **predators**, such as lions, because they need the grass to hide in as they stalk antelopes and other **prey**.

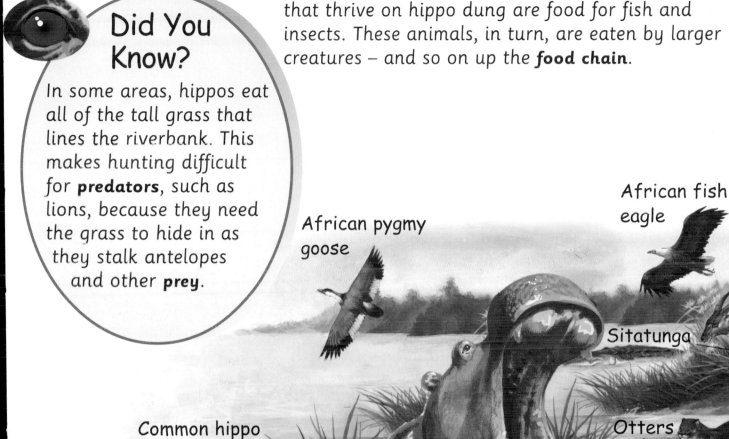

African pygmy goose

African fish eagle

Sitatunga

Common hippo

Otters

Dragonfly

Hippo facts

The ancient Egyptians believed one of the constellations (groups of stars visible in the night sky) was a hippo.

Adult hippos can stay underwater for more than 5 minutes.

Careless use of poisons endangers many animals. In Kenya, hippos have eaten plants treated with insecticides – chemicals used to stop insects from eating crops. These chemicals poisoned the hippos and then the animals that feed on their carcasses (dead bodies), including lions, hyenas and vultures.

Tourism is one of Africa's most important industries. Every year, thousands of visitors go to game parks to watch wildlife like elephants, rhinos, hippos and giraffes.

Tracking hippos in swamps is dangerous but quite easy. Just look for two deep ruts with a shallower, smoother dip in the middle. The ruts are made by the hippo's legs, the dip by its belly.

Hippos usually have just one baby at a time. Only very rarely do they have twins.

Female common hippos give birth every 18 months to 2 years. The babies are born about 34 weeks after mating. Pygmy hippos give birth after about 28 weeks.

Each school or group of hippos is very well organised. The babies stay close to their mothers or another adult female. As they grow, the young hippos play with others of the same age and sex. The males have mock fights and the females chase each other and roll around in the water.

If a male hippo comes into a crèche or shows signs of aggression near young hippos, the adult females attack him.

In areas where pygmy hippos have been hunted, they tend to hide in waterside vegetation and rarely come into the open.

Glossary

archaeologist Someone who studies the remains of past civilisations.

artiodactyl A mammal which has an even number of toes on each foot, but only walks on the third and fourth. These toes usually end in hooves or nails.

canine tooth Pointed tooth for tearing food.

crèche A group of young animals guarded by one or more adults.

ecosystem A group of organisms that depend on each other and their surroundings to survive.

food chain An arrangement of animals and plants in which each feeds on the one below it in the chain.

fossil The remains left by a plant or animal that lived long ago.

gland A body organ that produces a special substance.

habitat Wherever a plant or animal lives naturally.

herbivore An animal that eats only plants.

invertebrate An animal which has no backbone, such as a snail or worm.

mammal An animal that is born alive and then fed by its mother's milk.

muzzle The mouth, nose and jaw parts of some animals.

palaeontologist Someone who studies fossils and other ancient life forms.

papyrus A type of reed used by the ancient Egyptians to make boats and paper.

pharaoh The title of the rulers of ancient Egypt.

predator An animal that hunts and kills other animals for food.

prey An animal hunted and eaten by a predator.

secrete To produce and give off a substance, such as sweat.

species A group of animals or plants that look alike, live in the same way and produce young that do the same.

territory A piece of land that an animal or person defends against intruders.

tuber A thick underground stem or root of a plant.

Index